Lawyers
Jokes, Quotes, and Anecdotes

Lawyers
Jokes, Quotes, and Anecdotes

Edited by Patrick Regan

**Andrews McMeel
Publishing**

Kansas City

ISBN: 0-7407-1402-3

02 03 04 05 BIN 10 9 8 7 6 5 4 3 2

Library of Congress Catalog Card Number: 00-108468

Book design by Holly Camerlinck
Illustrations by Kevin Brimmer

Attention: Schools and Businesses

Andrews McMeel books are available at quantity discounts with bulk purchase
for educational, business, or sales promotional use. For information, please write to:
Special Sales Department, Andrews McMeel Publishing, 4520 Main Street,
Kansas City, Missouri 64111.

A lawyer's dream of Heaven:
Every man reclaimed his property at
the final resurrection, and each tried
to recover it from all his forefathers.

—Samuel Butler (1612–1680)

To me, a lawyer is basically the person
that knows the rules of the country. We're all
throwing the dice, playing the game, moving
our pieces around the board, but if there is
a problem, the lawyer is the only person
who has read the inside top of the box.

—Jerry Seinfeld

Introduction

Samuel Butler penned the witticism on the previous page in the mid-1600s. Jerry Seinfeld's quip is circa late twentieth century. The times may change, but lawyer jokes will always be around.

Why do we so love to make fun of lawyers and the law? Perhaps because it's so easy to do.

No place is so ripe for the picking as the halls of justice, and no target quite so tempting as the high-paid, argumentative folk who wander them. But lawyer jokes are just the beginning of what makes the litigious subphylum of our society such a rich source of humor. When it comes to legal matters, the facts are—in fact—often funnier than the fiction. In addition to hundreds of quotes and quips, this little book includes:

Strange but true local laws:

In Princeton, Texas, it's unlawful to throw onions at anyone.

In Carmel, California, it's illegal for a woman to bathe in a business office.

Hysterical but true statements pulled directly from trial transcripts:

LAWYER: Are you qualified to give a urine sample?

WITNESS: Yes. I have been since early childhood.

And wildly weird courtroom questions:

LAWYER: What happened then?

WITNESS: He told me . . . "I have to kill you because you can identify me."

LAWYER: Did he kill you?

Whether you work in our nation's legal system or do your darndest to stay out of it, you're sure to find plenty to surprise and amuse you in this little compendium of legal levity. The evidence is overwhelming, and the verdict is in . . . the law is worth its weight in laughs.

—*Patrick Regan*

If the laws could speak for themselves,
they would complain about the lawyers.

—*Sir George Savile*

The number of lawyers and personal
computers has increased greatly over the last
three decades. Unfortunately, the lawyers
haven't managed to get twice as fast and half
as expensive with each passing year.

A Texas attorney, realizing he was on the verge of unleashing a stupid question, interrupted himself and said, "Your Honor, I'd like to strike the next question."

All in all, I'd rather have been a judge than a miner. And what is more, being a miner, as soon as you are too old and tired and sick and stupid to do the job properly, you have to go. Well, the very opposite applies with the judges.

—*Peter Cook*

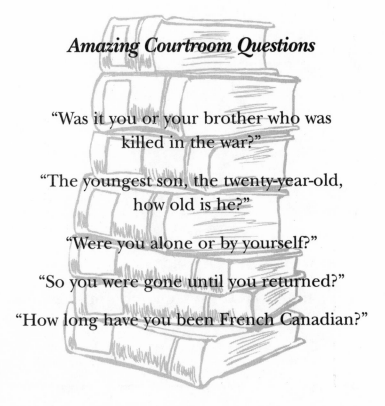

Amazing Courtroom Questions

"Was it you or your brother who was killed in the war?"

"The youngest son, the twenty-year-old, how old is he?"

"Were you alone or by yourself?"

"So you were gone until you returned?"

"How long have you been French Canadian?"

A plumber charged a law firm for repairs at the rate of $500. The lawyer who paid the bill was outraged. "Hey, even I don't charge that much! Isn't that a bit steep?" The plumber replied, "That's what I thought when I was a lawyer."

Any time a lawyer is seen and not heard, it's a shame to wake him.

A traveler in obvious distress made his way into a small town and stopped at the first store on Main Street. He stepped up to the counter and asked, "Does this town have a criminal attorney?" The clerk considered the question for a moment and then said, "Well, yes, we think so, but we haven't been able to prove it yet."

People who love sausage and respect the law should never watch either being made.

—*Otto von Bismarck*

A lawyer's dog, running about unleashed, snatched a roast from a butcher's market. The butcher hurried to the lawyer's office and asked, "If a dog is running around unleashed and steals a piece of meat from my store, do I have a right to demand payment for the meat from the dog's owner?"

The lawyer answered, "Absolutely."

"Your dog was loose and stole a roast from me today. You owe me $9.80."

The lawyer, without a word, wrote the butcher a check for $9.80. The next week, the butcher went to his mailbox to find a bill from the lawyer noting $50 for a consultation.

Lawyers

They say that talk is cheap—
until you get a lawyer involved.

A painter just coming from a job was stopped
by a police officer, who decided to request
a breath analysis. The painter was arrested for
having a blood alcohol level of .2 percent
and might have been convicted had it not
been discovered that the paint fumes were
registering as alcohol in the breath analysis.

—*Head and Joye,* 101 Ways to Avoid a Drunk Driving
Conviction *(Atlanta: Maximar Publishing, 1991)*

From Actual Court Records

Q: Doctor, did you say he was shot in the woods?
A: No. I said he was shot in the lumbar region.

Q: Doctor, as a result of your examination of the plaintiff, is the young lady pregnant?
A: The young lady is pregnant, but not as a result of my examination.

Q: You say that the stairs went down to the basement?
A: Yes.
Q: And these stairs, did they go up also?

People are getting smarter nowadays.
They are letting lawyers, instead of their
conscience, be their guides.

—*Will Rogers*

"You seem to be in some distress," said the
kindly judge to the witness. "Is anything the
matter?" "Well, Your Honor," said the witness,
"I swore to tell the truth, the whole truth,
and nothing but the truth, but every time
I try, some lawyer objects."

Strange but True

In Los Angeles, it's illegal to possess
a hippopotamus.

In Texas, it's illegal to put graffiti
on someone else's cow.

It's unlawful in both Ola, South Dakota,
and Anniston, Oklahoma, to lie down in the
middle of the road and take a nap.

In Willowdale, Oregon, a husband is prohibited from using profane language while making love to his wife.

It's illegal in Carmel, California, for a woman to bathe in a business office.

In Maryland, a man may not marry his wife's grandmother.

A grade-school teacher heard a child crying and rushed to the playground to see what was wrong. There, she found Trey, Kevin, and Phil—the latter crying furiously. When she asked what had happened, Trey told her, "Kevin took Phil's orange. Then Phil hit Kevin on the head and called him several dirty names, so Kevin kicked Phil in the stomach." The teacher replied, "Well, then, we'll all have to go to the principal's office. And where is the orange now?" Trey smiled and produced an orange from his pocket. "I have the orange. I'm Phil's lawyer."

A divorce lawyer is the person who referees
the fight and winds up with the purse.

"My whole family follows the medical
profession closely," the young man announced.
"They're lawyers."

The first thing we do, let's kill all the lawyers.

—A line from act 2 of William Shakespeare's Henry VI, *often mistaken as a contemptuous plan; in reality, the characters are plotting an anarchistic attempt to overthrow the king.*

A lawyer and an engineer were fishing in the Caribbean. The lawyer said, "I'm here because my house burned down, and everything I owned was destroyed by the fire. The insurance company paid for everything."

"That's quite a coincidence," said the engineer. "I'm here because my house and all my belongings were destroyed by a flood, and my insurance company also paid for everything."

The lawyer looked somewhat confused. "How do you start a flood?" he asked.

A jury is a collection of people banded together
to decide who hired the better lawyer.

Q: What's the difference between an
accountant and a lawyer?

A: Accountants know they're boring.

Following a distinguished legal career, a man arrived at the gates of Heaven, accompanied by the pope, who had the misfortune to expire on the same day. The pope was greeted first by St. Peter, who escorted him to his quarters. The room was somewhat shabby and small, similar to that found in a low-grade motel. The lawyer was then taken to his room, which was a palatial suite including a private swimming pool, a garden, and a terrace overlooking the gates. The attorney was somewhat taken aback and told St. Peter, "I'm really quite surprised at these rooms, seeing as how the pope was given such small accommodations." St. Peter replied, "We have over a hundred popes here, and we're really very bored with them. We've never had a lawyer."

From Actual Court Records

Q: Please state the nature of your relationship to the minor child.

A: I'm his mother.

Q: And you have been so all of his life?

Q: And where did he give you those injections?

A: In his office.

Q: And that's exactly correct. Indeed he did. What part of your . . .

A: I'm sorry.

Q: No, no, you're right. What part of your body did he inject?

The lawyer wandered home at three in the morning. His wife became very upset, telling him, "You're late! You said you'd be home by 11:45!" The lawyer replied, "I'm right on time. I said I'd be home by a quarter of twelve."

Did you hear about the woman who sent out 1,500 perfumed erotic valentines signed, "Guess who?"
She's a divorce lawyer.

A new attorney, absorbed in his presentation, spoke to the jury hour upon hour, meandering through points unrelated to the case. When he finally yielded the floor, his experienced opponent approached the jury, spread her hands, and said simply, "I have decided to imitate my noble adversary and submit the case to you without an argument."

A woman found a bottle on a beach. When she opened the stopper, out flew a genie. "I am the Genie of Lawyers," he said. "I will grant you three wishes, but know that lawyers everywhere will have your wish, only doubled." "Okay, for my first wish, I want $10 million," she said. "Done, and every lawyer just got twenty," said the genie. "And I've always wanted a home in the south of France," she said. "You have one, and they all have two," said the genie. "And finally, I've always wanted to donate a kidney for transplant."

Under Oath . . .

JUDGE: Is your appearance this morning pursuant to a deposition notice, which I sent to your attorney?

DEFENDANT: No. This is how I always dress when I go to work.

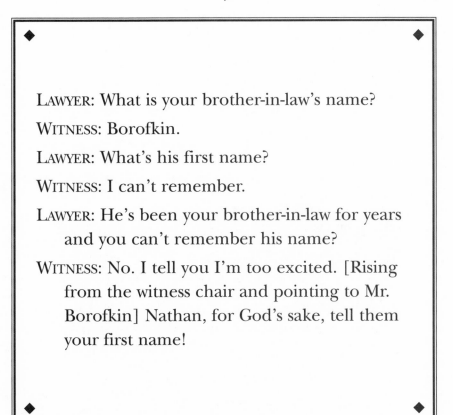

LAWYER: What is your brother-in-law's name?

WITNESS: Borofkin.

LAWYER: What's his first name?

WITNESS: I can't remember.

LAWYER: He's been your brother-in-law for years and you can't remember his name?

WITNESS: No. I tell you I'm too excited. [Rising from the witness chair and pointing to Mr. Borofkin] Nathan, for God's sake, tell them your first name!

A lawyer and a priest were traveling together. The priest, by way of conversation, asked, "Do you make mistakes in court?" "Rarely," came the haughty reply. "If they are large, I correct them. If small, I let them go. Do you make mistakes in the pulpit?"

"Sometimes," was the reply. "And I handle them the way you do. Last Sunday I meant to tell the congregation that the Devil was the Father of Lies, but it came out Father of Lawyers. But it was small, so I let it go."

The minute you
read something you
can't understand,
you can be
almost sure it was
drawn up by
a lawyer.

—*Will Rogers*

Law and order is like patriotism—anyone
who comes on strong about patriotism has
got something to hide; it never fails.
They always turn out to be a crook or
an [ass] or a traitor or something.

—*Bill Mauldin*

Having lawyers make laws is like
having doctors make diseases.

In 1990, Dr. James M. Dabbs Jr., a psychologist with Georgia State University, revealed that high levels of testosterone—which causes overly aggressive or antisocial behavior—is commonly found in juvenile delinquents, substance abusers, bullies, dropouts, and trial lawyers.

He reminds me of the man who murdered both his parents and then, when sentence was about to be pronounced, pleaded for mercy on the grounds that he was an orphan.

—*Attributed to Abraham Lincoln*

A junior partner in a law firm was sent
to a far-away country to represent a long-term
client accused of robbery. After days of trial,
the case was won, and the client was acquitted
and released. Excited about his success,
the attorney wired the firm, "Justice prevailed."
The senior partner wired back in haste,
"Appeal immediately."

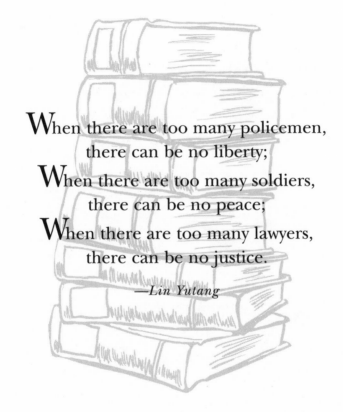

When there are too many policemen,
there can be no liberty;
When there are too many soldiers,
there can be no peace;
When there are too many lawyers,
there can be no justice.

—*Lin Yutang*

Lawyers have been known to wrest from reluctant juries triumphant verdicts of acquittal for their clients, even when those clients, as often happens, were clearly and unmistakably innocent.

—*Oscar Wilde*

A man may as well open an oyster without a knife, as a lawyer's mouth without a fee.

—*Barten Holyday*

Clinton has conducted the opening weeks
of his presidency in a lawyerly way,
getting bogged down in technicalities,
loopholes, caveats, and flyspecking.

—New York Times

I don't want a lawyer to tell me what
I cannot do; I hire him to tell me how
to do what I want to do.

—*J. P. Morgan*

A lawyer lay dying, with his partner of forty years by his bedside. "Jack, I've got to confess. I've been sleeping with your wife for thirty years and I'm the father of your daughter, Hillary. On top of that, I've been stealing from the firm for a decade." "Relax," says Jack, "and don't think another thing about it. I'm the one who put arsenic in your martini."

Poetic Legal Advice

You can say it with flowers,

You can say it with candy,

You can say it with jewelry or drink.

You can say it with candles and dinner with brandy,

But be sure you don't say it with ink.

A doctor, an engineer, and a lawyer were arguing over whose was the oldest profession. The doctor asserted that, of course, a physician removed Adam's rib to create Eve. The engineer disagreed and said, "Of course, an engineer had to have constructed the Garden of Eden."

"I have you both beaten," the lawyer gloated. "Before Adam and Eve, before the Garden of Eden, before all creation, there was a state of chaos, and who do you think could have created that?"

A vengeful man came to lawyer Abe Lincoln asking him to sue a man who was living in poverty for $2.50. When Lincoln couldn't dissuade the fellow, he charged him $10 as a legal fee. Lincoln gave half of that to the defendant, who openly confessed to the debt and paid the $2.50, settling the dispute agreeably.

A golfer hooked his tee shot over a hill and onto the next fairway. Walking toward his ball, he saw a man lying on the ground, groaning with pain.

"I'm an attorney," the wincing man said, "and this is going to cost you $5,000."

"I'm sorry, I'm really sorry," the concerned golfer replied. "But I did yell, 'fore!'"

"I'll take it!" the attorney said.

A lawyer in her start-up office wanted to impress the first client, who was just walking in the door. She picked up the phone and announced loudly, "Well, I regret having to tell you this, but I have a huge caseload and won't be able to investigate that for another month." She hung up and asked the visitor, "May I help you?"

The man put down his case and said, "Don't need no help. Just came to hook up the phone."

For certain people after fifty,
litigation takes the place of sex.

—Gore Vidal

An astute lawyer once said, "A judge should
be about sixty years old, clean-shaven with
white hair, have sea-blue eyes, and suffer
with hemorrhoids so that he will have
that concerned look."

I have knowingly defended a number
of guilty men. But the guilty never
escape unscathed. My fees are sufficient
punishment for anyone.

—*F. Lee Bailey*

If you think that you can think about a
thing inextricably attached to something else,
without thinking of the thing it is attached to,
then you have a legal mind.

—*Thomas Reed Powell*

A woman was being questioned in a court trial involving slander. "Please repeat the slanderous statements you heard, exactly as you heard them," instructed the lawyer. The witness hesitated. "But they are unfit for any respectable person to hear," she protested. "Then," said the attorney, "just whisper them to the judge."

Children are innocent and love justice, while most adults are wicked and prefer mercy.

—*G. K. Chesterton*

A witness called upon to testify about a head-on collision was asked, "Whose fault was this accident?"

He replied, "It's hard to say. As nearly as I could tell, they hit each other at about the same time."

Lawyers are: Those who earn a living by the sweat of their brow-beating.

—*James G. Huneker*

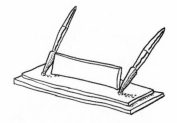

After successfully trying her case, Clarence Darrow was embraced by his lovely client, who thanked him expansively and desired to know, "How can I ever thank you?"

"My dear," replied the lawyer, "ever since the Phoenicians invented money, there has only been one answer to that question."

Beneath this smooth stone
   by the bone of his bone
Sleeps Master John Gill;
   By lies when alive
      this attorney did thrive,
And now that he's dead
   he lies still.

   —Tombstone epitaph,
   Massachusetts churchyard

Strange but True

One man's will read: "To my wife, I leave her lover, and the knowledge that I was not the fool she thought me; to my son I leave the pleasure of earning a living. For twenty years he thought the pleasure mine. He was mistaken."

When he died in 1927, Canadian lawyer Charles Millar bequeathed $568,000 "to the mother who has given birth in Toronto to the greatest number of children" during the ten years after his death.

Newspapers labeled the resulting "competition" the Stork Derby. The will was bitterly contested for twelve years, but eventually the money was divided among four women who each had produced nine children in the allotted time.

One winner then announced her future support of birth control.

A lawyer was discussing her legal strategy with a client and told him, "Now, when I approach the jury with my final remarks, I'll also plead for clemency."

"You'll do nothing of the kind!" shouted the fellow. "Let Clemency get his own lawyer!"

In the Halls of Justice the only justice is in the halls.

—*Lenny Bruce*

A red-faced judge convened court after a long lunch. The first case involved a man charged with drunk driving who claimed it simply wasn't true. "I'm as sober as you are, Your Honor," the man claimed. The judge replied, "Clerk, please enter a guilty plea. The defendant is sentenced to thirty days."

Question: Officer, what led you to believe the defendant was under the influence?
Answer: Because he was argumentary and he couldn't pronunciate his words.

Under Oath . . .

LAWYER: Did you ever stay all night with this man
  in New York?

WITNESS: I refuse to answer that question.

LAWYER: Did you ever stay all night with this man
  in Chicago?

WITNESS: I refuse to answer that question.

LAWYER: Did you ever stay all night with this man
  in Miami?

WITNESS: No.

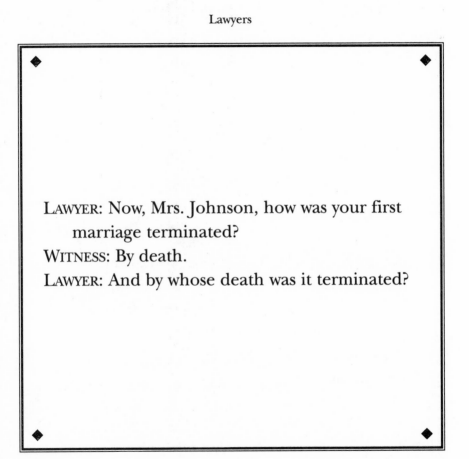

LAWYER: Now, Mrs. Johnson, how was your first
   marriage terminated?
WITNESS: By death.
LAWYER: And by whose death was it terminated?

In Japan there are about 12 lawyers for every 100,000 people. In Germany, there are 82 for every 100,000. In England, there are almost 103 for that same number, and in the United States there are nearly 308 lawyers per 100,000 residents.

—Ed Rubenstein, "Punitive Damages," National Review, *November 4, 1991*

The Holocaust was an obscene period
in our nation's history. I mean this
century's history. But we all lived in
this century. I didn't live in this century.

—*Dan Quayle, attorney*

The defendant who pleads his own case has a
fool for a client, but at least there won't be a
problem with fee splitting.

After a grueling yearlong search, a frustrated U.S. marshal finally caught up with a bank robber in his native town south of the border. He sidled up behind the bandit in a cantina, drew his gun, and said, "You're under arrest. Tell me where you stashed the cash or I'll blow you away." The criminal didn't speak English, so a lawyer standing nearby offered to interpret. "Tell him where you put the money or he'll shoot," the lawyer advised in Spanish. The bandit quickly gave the nearby location where he'd buried the money. "What did he say?" asked the marshal. "He said, 'Take a hike, jerk, you don't have the guts to kill me.'"

One juror to another: "I guess you noticed
that neither the prosecutor nor the
defense attorney swore to tell the truth."

A law firm is successful when it has
more clients than partners.

—*Henny Youngman*

Two sojourners in a hot air balloon lost their way and needed to get some direction. They dropped altitude and cruised along the treetops until they spotted a man jogging through the countryside. "Hey," yelled one, "can you give us our location?" "You're in a hot air balloon about ninety feet in the air!" the jogger called back. The first balloonist remarked, "That's a lawyer." "How do you know?" asked the second. "Because he gave us completely accurate and certain information that didn't help us in the slightest."

Legislation in the United States is a
digestive process by Congress with frequent
regurgitations by the Supreme Court.

—Attributed to Sir Wilmot Lewis

Two very rich people got divorced, and their
lawyers lived happily ever after.

How many lawyers does it take
to change a flat tire?

Three: One to call the tow truck on the
cell phone, one to stir the martinis, and
one to take notes for the upcoming
lawsuit against the tire company.

If there were no bad people,
there would be no good lawyers.

—*David Cort*

An Irish attorney was making the best of a shaky case when the judge interrupted him on a point of law.

"Surely your clients are aware of the doctrine *de minimis non curat lex?*"

"I assure you, my lord," came the suave reply, "that in the remote hamlet where my clients have their humble abode, it forms the sole topic of conversation."

—*Walter Bryan, "The Improbable Irish"*

A top partner in a major Chicago law firm charged clients for 6,022 billable hours for 1993. That would mean that the attorney worked sixteen and a half hours each day, every single day of the year. His billable rate the year before was $350 per hour.

—Wall Street Journal, *May 27, 1994*

How many lawyers does it take to change a lightbulb?

How many can you afford?

I saw a senator on a Sunday morning
talk show who said actions of the Senate
have created jobs for a lot of citizens.
Yeah, let's face it—you can't make a
career out of jury duty.

—*Jay Leno*

When the government puts teeth in the law,
they aren't always wisdom teeth.

A lawyer's dream of Heaven:
Every man reclaimed his property at the final
resurrection, and each tried to recover it
from all his forefathers.

—*Samuel Butler*

The term "Blue Laws" began in 1665 when
a clergyman and a governor of the New Haven
Colony determined a strict legal code of
personal conduct and produced the
document on blue paper.

Doctors and lawyers must go to school
for years and years, often with little sleep
and with great sacrifice to their
first wives.

—*Roy Blount*

Crime is only the retail department of what,
in wholesale, we call penal law.

—*George Bernard Shaw*

Looney Laws

You cannot walk down the street with
your shoelaces untied in Maine.

It is against the law to throw snowballs
in Oklahoma City, Oklahoma.

Lollipop sales are forbidden in
Spokane, Washington.

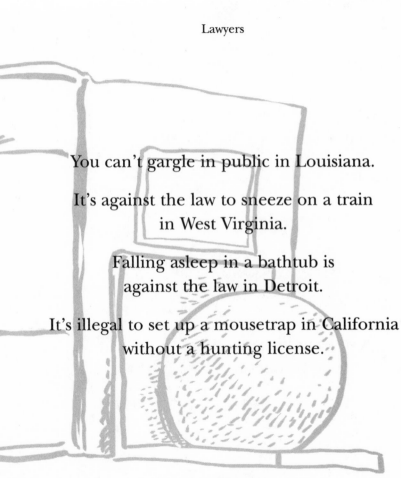

You can't gargle in public in Louisiana.

It's against the law to sneeze on a train
in West Virginia.

Falling asleep in a bathtub is
against the law in Detroit.

It's illegal to set up a mousetrap in California
without a hunting license.

Q: What's the difference between a lawyer and an orthodontist?

A: You get your money's worth from the orthodontist's retainer.

A peasant between two lawyers is like a fish between two cats.

—*Spanish proverb*

A woman in court confronted her attacker, pointing to him and shouting, "That's him! I'd know that face anywhere!"

"No way, lady," the thug sneered. "You couldn't recognize me, I was wearing a mask."

There was a time when an apple a day kept the doctor away, but now it's malpractice insurance.

Strange but True

In 1931, a Missouri district attorney offered a few ideas about the appropriate punishment for a man he was prosecuting: "He ought to be shot through the mouth of a red-hot cannon, through a barbed-wire fence, and into the jaws of hell before being kicked in the seat of the pants by a Missouri mule and thrown into a manure pile to rot."

In 1996, a man told a Zimbabwe court that he had sex with a cow because he was afraid of contracting AIDS from a human partner.

In his will, W. C. Fields left $10,000 to his wife, Harriet. To his mistress, Carlotta Monti, he bequeathed $25,000, a dictionary, two bottles of perfume, and a Cadillac.

On changing a plea from not guilty to guilty,
the judge asked the defendant for the reason.
"I didn't know there'd be women on the jury,"
he replied. "If I can't fool one woman,
I certainly can't fool six of them."

Our court dockets are so overcrowded
today that it would be better to call it
overdue process of law.

—*Bill Vaughn*

The new lawyer approached the bench at the judge's indication. "Have you ever been up before me?" he asked.

I don't know," was the reply. "What time do you get up?"

Bumper sticker wisdom:
Support your local lawyer; send your kid to medical school.

Most good
lawyers
live well,
work hard,
and die poor.

—*Daniel Webster*

An attorney sued a meditation guru
because, after eleven years, his client still
had never achieved the "perfect state of life"
he'd been promised. The lawyer was
awarded more than $137,000 in damages.

He was a lawyer, yet not a rascal,
and the people were astonished.

—*Said of St. Ives, thirteenth-century lawyer and saint*

There's a new word processing
software program for attorneys.
You can change the font, but when you
print it out the words always show up
in fine print.

Of the first forty-two U.S. presidents,
twenty-six were lawyers.

From Actual Court Records

ATTORNEY: Then there's a minus $85,000 plus interest. What did you believe that referenced when you signed it?

WITNESS: Creative financing.

ATTORNEY: But seriously, folks.

Q: I show you Exhibit 3 and ask if you recognize that picture.

A: That's me.

Q: Were you present when that picture was taken?

We have an insanity plea that
would have saved Cain.

—*Mark Twain*

In the wee hours of the morning,
a lawyer called the governor of his state
to inform him that a noted judge had
just died and the lawyer wanted to take
the judge's place. The irritated governor
wickedly assured him, "If it's okay with
the funeral parlor, it's okay with me."

A man was trapped behind the wheel of a burning car. "Give me your hand!" insisted a heroic bystander. The man remained gripped in fear at the wheel. "C'mon, give us your hand!" several people tried to coax him, to no avail. A colleague of the man happened upon the scene and heard the commotion. He put his head in the car and said, "Take my hand!" and hauled the man out in the nick of time. "How did you know what to say?" they asked him. "He's an IRS attorney," he replied. "Don't ask him to give you anything."

An older attorney took a freshly graduated
lawyer to lunch and gave her this advice:
"The most important thing you can do as a
lawyer is to be sincere. Sincerity, sincerity
at all times. Whether you mean it or not."

Between grand theft and a legal fee
there only stands a law degree.

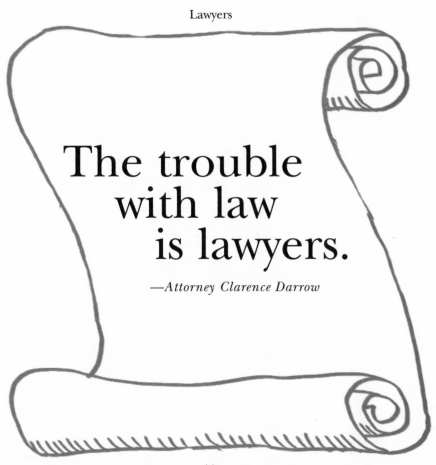

The trouble with law is lawyers.

—Attorney Clarence Darrow

Two lawyers were standing in line at their
bank when armed robbers burst in.
One robber began gathering money from
the tellers, and the other shoved the
customers to the wall and proceeded
to take their wallets and valuables. The first
lawyer in line turned to the other and
thrust $50 into his hand. "What's this?"
the surprised fellow asked. The first answered,
"It's that fifty bucks I owe you."

Another name for divorce:
An antitrust suit.

"If the law supposes that," said Mr. Bumble,
"then the law is a ass, a idiot."

—*From* Oliver Twist *by Charles Dickens*

An attorney in heaven, unhappy with her circumstances, complained to St. Peter, who told her she'd have to appeal, and that would take three years. Taking the attorney aside, the devil whispered that she could have a hearing in two days if the attorney would change the venue to hell. When the attorney asked why appeals could be heard so much sooner in hell, the devil laughed, "We have all the judges."

The more numerous the laws,
the more corrupt the state.

—*Tacitus*

I don't think you can make a lawyer
honest by an act of legislature. You've got
to work on his conscience. And his lack
of conscience is what makes him a lawyer.

—*Will Rogers*

A lawyer and a doctor, each in a Mercedes, were driving toward each other on a winding road one dark night when they sideswiped each other. Neither was hurt, but both were really rattled by the accident. The lawyer pulled a flask from his coat and offered the doctor a calming swallow. The doctor took a long pull from the bottle and handed it back to the lawyer, who put it away. "Aren't you having one?" he asked. "You bet," said the lawyer, "right after the patrol officer fills out his report."

There are two kinds of lawyers:
Those who know the law and those
who know the judge.

Alimony is like buying oats
for a dead horse.

—Arthur Baer

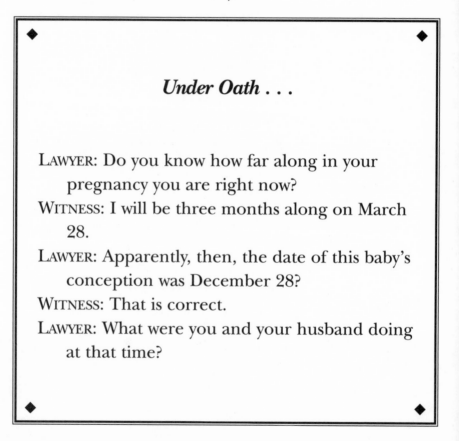

Under Oath . . .

LAWYER: Do you know how far along in your pregnancy you are right now?

WITNESS: I will be three months along on March 28.

LAWYER: Apparently, then, the date of this baby's conception was December 28?

WITNESS: That is correct.

LAWYER: What were you and your husband doing at that time?

LAWYER: How did you happen to choose Dr. McCarthy as your physician?

WITNESS: Well, I know a woman across town who told me she'd had several of her children by Dr. McCarthy, and she said he was really good.

LAWYER: And finally, all your responses must be oral. Understood? What school do you go to?

WITNESS: Oral.

LAWYER: How old are you?

WITNESS: Oral.

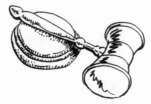

A gang of bank robbers mistakenly broke
into a lawyers' club and the old fellows
gave them the fight of their lives.
The thieves were glad to get away before
the police arrived. "Not so bad," said one
thief to the others. "We got out with
fifty bucks between us." "Fool!"
shouted the boss. "We went in there
with over a hundred!"

It is hard to say whether the doctors of law
or the doctors of divinity have made
the greater advances in the lucrative
business of mystery.

—*Samuel Goldwyn*

A tough trial attorney lost for the defense
in a burglary conviction. His panicky client
turned to him and asked, "So, Counselor,
where do we go from here?" The old trial
dog replied, "Son, you're going to jail.
I'm going to lunch."

When the attorney learned that his colleague of thirty years was dying, he hurried to the hospital. He found his friend struggling through page after page of Holy Scripture. "Looking for solace, my friend?" he asked compassionately. "Nope," the dying man replied, "loopholes."

Deals aren't usually blown by principles; they're blown by lawyers and accountants trying to prove how valuable they are.

—*Robert Townsend*

JUDGE: Have you ever stolen?

THIEF: Oh, off and on.

JUDGE: What did you steal?

THIEF: Oh, this and that.

JUDGE: Officer, take him to his cell.

THIEF: Hey, when do I get out?

JUDGE: Oh, sooner or later.

Strange but True

In Kentucky, it's against the law to use
reptiles during religious services.

Hot Springs, Arkansas, forbids
gurgling in public.

In the coastal provinces of Canada it is illegal
to shoot a whale from a moving automobile.

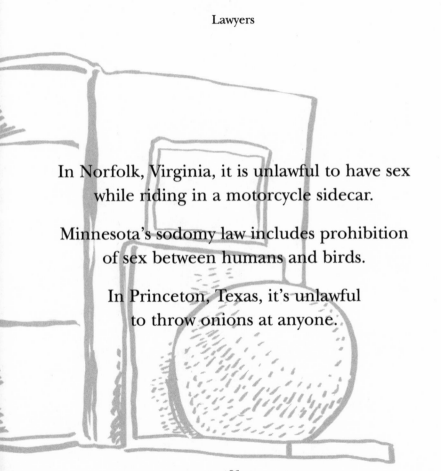

In Norfolk, Virginia, it is unlawful to have sex
while riding in a motorcycle sidecar.

Minnesota's sodomy law includes prohibition
of sex between humans and birds.

In Princeton, Texas, it's unlawful
to throw onions at anyone.

Q: What's the difference between a lawyer and a boxing referee?

A: A boxing referee doesn't get paid more for a longer fight.

How does a pregnant woman know she is carrying a lawyer-to-be?

She finds she craves baloney.

Law school taught me one thing:
How to take two situations that are exactly
the same and show how they are different.

—*Hart Pomerantz*

How many lawyers does it take
to change a lightbulb?

Three. One to climb the ladder, one to shake
the ladder, and one to sue the ladder company.

JUDGE: It says that the charge is theft of frozen chickens. Are you the defendant, sir?
DEFENDANT: No, Your Honor, I'm the guy who stole the chickens.

When you go to court, you are putting your fate into the hands of twelve people who weren't smart enough to get out of jury duty.

—*Norm Crosby*

A lawyer named Strange selected his future tombstone and told the monument company that he wanted "Here lies an honest man and a lawyer" cut into the stone. "Can't do that," said the stone cutter, "because it's illegal to bury two people in one plot. But I could say very simply, 'Here lies an honest lawyer.'" "Then people wouldn't know it was me," worried Mr. Strange. "'Course they would, sir. They'd go by, read the words, and say, 'That's Strange.'"

A terminally ill man called his physician to his bedside and asked, "How long have I got?"

"I doubt you'll live through the night," murmured the healer.

"Then call my lawyer," directed the man. When the attorney arrived, the dying man asked the two men to stand on either side of the bed. When they inquired why they should flank the patient, he replied, "Jesus died with thieves on either side of Him. I thought I'd like to go out the same way."

Lawyers sometimes tell the truth.
They'll do anything to win a case.

—*Jeremy Bentham*

"The doctor is in the courtroom on
Tuesdays and Wednesdays."

—*Overheard at a physician's office*

————◆◆◆————

During the cross-examination of a coroner at a murder trial, the prosecution asked, "Did you take the victim's pulse before you pronounced him dead?"

"No."

"Did you check his breathing?"

"No."

"So you didn't make any of the usual tests to be sure the man was dead?"

"Look at it this way: All I had to examine was a brain in a jar, but for all I know, he may still be out there somewhere practicing law."

————◆◆◆————

A lawyer is the only person
in the courtroom whose ignorance
of the law goes unpunished.

If you took all the laws and laid them
end to end, there would be no end.

—*Mark Twain*

A teacher, a garbage collector, and a lawyer appeared in Heaven at the same time. St. Peter was having a bad day because of overcrowding, so when they got to the gate, Peter decided there would be a test to get in.

For the teacher's question, St. Peter asked, "What was the name of the famous ship that was sunk by an iceberg with most of its passengers?" "The *Titanic*," the teacher answered, and Peter let him in.

Peter's mood was getting darker at the thought of smelly overalls in Heaven, so he asked the garbage collector a harder question, "And how many people died on the ship?" The garbage man guessed "1,523." It happened to be right, and he was admitted.

Finally St. Peter turned to the lawyer and said, "Name them."

The judge questioned the witness, "Do you understand that you are on trial for murder?" "Yes," replied the defendant. "Do you understand the penalty for perjury?" "I most certainly do," was the answer, "and it's a lot less than the penalty for murder."

The term "red tape" comes from nineteenth-century England when documents were bound in reddish ribbon. Common folk derisively cited the process of tying and untying the tape as an excuse for the slowness of government decisions.

Painters and lawyers can soon change
white to black.

The judge questioned the witness, "Do you
understand that you have sworn to tell the
truth?"

"I do," was the reply.

"And do you understand what will happen if
you are not truthful?"

"You bet," came the reply. "My side wins."

A man's respect for law and order
exists in precise relationship to the size
of his paycheck.

—*Adam Clayton Powell Jr.*

One doesn't need a brain to be a lawyer,
only a cast-iron bottom.

—*"Old Bull" Warren*

A salesman harassed W. C. Fields until the actor ducked into a barbershop to avoid him. The tenacious fellow went in as well, and Fields yelled in exasperation, "I've told you no ten times now. Just to shut you up, I'll put the proposition to my lawyer next time I see him!"

The salesman pressed, "Will you take the proper steps if he says it's all right?"

"I certainly will," announced Fields. "I'll ask another lawyer."

A situation every lawyer dreads:
An open-and-shut case with no insurance
on the other side.

Until 10,000 years ago, lawyers wandered
about in small tribes, seeking clients.
Finally small settlements of lawyers began to
spring up in the Ur Valley, the birthplace of
modern civilization. With settlement came
the invention of writing.

—*From* A Short History of Lawyers *by Hugh L. Dewey, Esq.*

It's been said that there are only
four actual jokes about lawyers.
All the rest are truisms.

Definition of legal justice:
A decision in your favor.

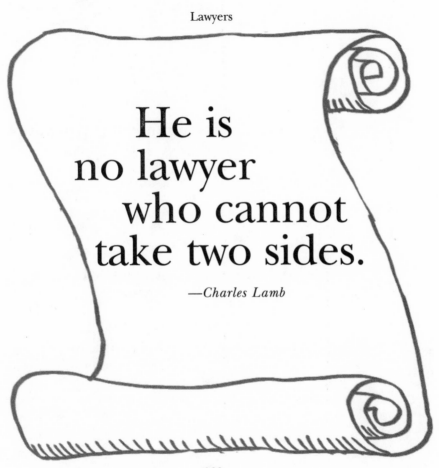

He is
no lawyer
who cannot
take two sides.

—Charles Lamb

Q: How was copper wire invented?

A: Two lawyers arguing over a penny.

A man who never graduated from school
might steal from a freight car. But a man
who attends college and graduates as
a lawyer might steal the whole railroad.

—*President Theodore Roosevelt,*
persuading his son to become a lawyer

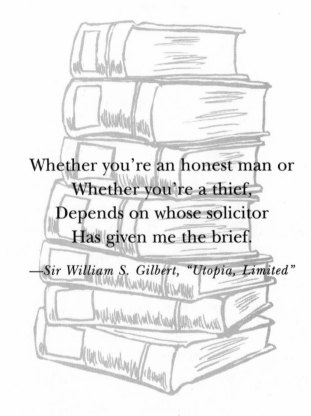

Whether you're an honest man or
Whether you're a thief,
Depends on whose solicitor
Has given me the brief.

—Sir William S. Gilbert, "Utopia, Limited"

Dim lights

Q: How many lawyers does it take
to change a lightbulb?

A: Such number as may be deemed necessary to perform the stated task in a timely and efficient manner within the strictures of the following agreement: Whereas the party of the first part, also known as "Lawyer," and the party of the second part, also known as "Lightbulb," do hereby and forthwith agree to a transaction wherein the party of the second part (Lightbulb) shall be removed from the current position. The aforementioned removal transaction shall include, but not be limited to, the following steps:

1) The party of the first part (Lawyer) shall, with or without elevation at his option, by means of a chair, stepstool, ladder, or any other means of elevation, grasp the party of the second part (Lightbulb) and rotate the party of the second part (Lightbulb) in a counter-clockwise direction, this point being nonnegotiable.

2) Upon reaching a point where the party of the second part (Lightbulb) becomes separated from the party of the third part (Receptacle), the party of the first part (Lawyer) shall have the option of disposing of the party of the second part (Lightbulb) in a manner consistent with all applicable state, local, and federal statutes.

As we watched Judge Clarence Thomas's
Supreme Court confirmation hearings,
all of the commentators said the same thing:
"One of these people in the room is lying."
Do you believe that? You've got two lawyers and
fourteen senators in the room, and only
one of them is lying?

—*Jay Leno*

Lawyers spend a great deal of their
time shoveling smoke.

—*Oliver Wendall Holmes*

The United States is the only country in the
world where the court lets the prisoner go
home and locks up the jury.

A man received his property tax bill only days before it was due, and to vent his frustration wrote "Bob Wade, Bastard" instead of "Bob Wade, County Treasurer" on the envelope. He also included an obscene message. Wade filed a libel suit against the taxpayer. The defendant argued that public officials should be able to take a little guff, but the judge didn't agree. He fined the defendant double what he'd paid in taxes.

Laws are always useful to those
who possess and vexatious to those
who have nothing.

—*Rousseau*

"I told you that you should've got yourself
some legal advice before running
to a lawyer."

—*Overheard in a courthouse corridor*

Amazing Courtroom Confessions

"The pedestrian had no idea which direction to go, so I ran over him."

"The other car collided with mine without giving warning of its intentions."

"I pulled away from the side of the road, glanced at my mother-in-law, and headed over the embankment."

"The guy was all over the road. I had to swerve several times before I hit him."

If they ever give you a brief, attack the medical evidence. Remember, the jury's full of rheumatism and arthritis and shocking gastric troubles. They love to see a medical man put through it.

—John Mortimer, advising law students

International Laws Governing Romance (some no longer observed): You can send a love letter at half the postal rate in Venezuela if it is enclosed in a red envelope.

Strange but True

It is illegal to kiss someone who is not a relative in Egypt.

A job seeker's résumé included this nugget: "Failed bar exam with relatively high grades."

A man sentenced to be hanged in
France can be saved by marriage to a willing,
virtuous maiden.

When a woman gives birth in Japan, the
father must get into the bed and simulate labor.
In that same country, all public demonstrations
of affection are outlawed. Kissing a girl
can result in a jail sentence.

Under Oath . . .

Directive from the judge's bench: Now, as
we begin, I must ask you to banish all present
information and prejudice from your minds,
if you have any.

LAWYER: What happened then?
WITNESS: He told me, he says, "I have to kill you
    because you can identify me."
LAWYER: Did he kill you?

LAWYER: Do you believe that you are emotionally unstable?

WITNESS: I should certainly think so.

LAWYER: How many times have you committed suicide?

WITNESS: Four times.

After sentencing a man to jail, the judge pointed his cane at the offender and remarked to the court, "At the end of this stick is a scalawag."

"There certainly is," said the convict, "but he's not the one at this end."

When you have no basis for argument, abuse the plaintiff.

—*Cicero*

Two lawyers were out hunting when they came upon some tracks. The first declared they were deer tracks. The other insisted they were elk tracks. They were still arguing when the train hit them.

I have nothing but utter contempt for the courts of this land.

—*George C. Wallace*

Looney Laws

It's against the law to water a garden if it's raining in Montreal.

Public kissing is only legal in railroad stations in Italy.

In China, it's illegal to save a drowning person, as that would interfere with his or her fate.

It's against the law to wear white shoes in Tibet.

In London, it's legal to be nude in a theater as long as one sits perfectly still. However, it is illegal to kiss a girl on Sunday in that same city.

It's a crime to employ a woman under the age of forty-five as a chorus girl in Australia.

About 75 percent of those taking the bar
in this country pass it. In Japan, only
2 percent pass the bar.

—New Jersey Law Journal, *June 22, 1992*

The Los Angeles Central Criminal Division
disposed of 474 felony preliminary hearings
in the time it took to dispose of the
O. J. Simpson preliminary hearing.

—USA Today, *July 12, 1994*

A judge opened court with this announcement: "The lawyer for the defense has paid me $15,000 to decide for his client. The lawyer for plaintiff paid me $10,000 to hold favorably for the case she made. In the interest of a fair trial, I am returning $5,000 to the defense."

Strange but True

In 1993, two Ohio prison inmates sued
General Foods. They complained that the
company failed to tell them that Maxwell
House coffee is addictive, and they demanded
compensation for the headaches and
insomnia they suffered in prison.

In 1996, a truck driver filed a $10 million lawsuit after receiving a defective penile transplant. The complainant said he suffered blisters, bruising, infection, and embarrassment. "He could be just walking down the street," his attorney added, "and it would erect on its own."

In 1857, England established a court for divorce and matrimonial cases. Men could divorce on the grounds of adultery alone. Women were required to prove not only adultery but further abuses, such as rape, bestiality, or incest.

We don't seem to be able to even check crime, so why not legalize it and put a heavy tax on it . . . We have taxed other industries out of business—it might work here.

—*Will Rogers*

"I have come to the conclusion that one useless man is called a disgrace, two are called a law firm, and three or more become a Congress."

—*The character of John Adams in the play* 1776

Lawyers,
I suppose,
were
children
once.

—*Charles Lamb*

The United States has 5 percent of the
world's population and 70 percent
of the lawyers.

—Business Insurance, *January 27, 1992*

Some people think about sex all the time;
some people think of sex some of the time;
and some people never think about sex:
They become lawyers.

—*Woody Allen*

Top Thirteen Law-Related Films

(as judged by the authors of *Reel Justice*)

Anatomy of a Murder
Breaker Morant
The Caine Mutiny
Fury
Inherit the Wind
Judgment at Nuremberg
Libel
The Life of Emile Zola
A Man for All Seasons
My Cousin Vinny
To Kill a Mockingbird
Twelve Angry Men
Witness for the Prosecution

———◆◆◆———

Asked to officiate at a friend's wedding ceremony, Justice Felix Frankfurter explained that he did not have the authority to perform the ceremony.

"What!" exclaimed his friend. "A Supreme Court justice doesn't have the authority to marry people!? How come?"

"I guess," replied Frankfurter, "it's because marriage is not considered a federal offense."

———◆◆◆———

A doctor told his patient that she only had six months to live. The distraught patient asked the doctor what she could possibly do to have more time. The doctor advised, "Marry a lawyer. It will be the longest six months of your life."

A doctor vacationing on the beach saw a fin
emerge from the surf and promptly fainted.
His wife revived him and admonished,
"Darling, you've got to stop imagining
you are seeing lawyers everywhere."

There is no better way to exercise
the imagination than the study of law.
No artist ever interpreted nature as freely
as a lawyer interprets the truth.

—*Jean Giradoux*

A small-town lawyer made a
modest living until another lawyer
moved into his town. Then they both
made a fortune.

Nothing could be more boring
than an absolutely accurate movie
about the law.

—*Roger Ebert*

There's a new sushi bar in town
that is especially attractive to lawyers.
It's called "Sosumi."

BYSTANDER: Did your lawyer give you bad advice?
PLAINTIFF: No. I paid for it.

The patent attorney turned from
his office window with the invention
in his hand and complained to the inventor,
"Death ray, my ass. It hardly slowed
them down."

I was never ruined but twice.
Once when I lost a lawsuit and
once when I gained one.

—*Voltaire*

Courts of law met in the dark in
ancient Egypt so that the judge could
remain impartial, not seeing the defendant,
accuser, or witnesses.

FIRST LAWYER: As soon as I learned the business
was crooked, I got out of it.
SECOND LAWYER: How much?

During Jury Selection

ATTORNEY: Have you heard anything about this
case?

CANDIDATE: No.

ATTORNEY: Have you read anything about this
case?

CANDIDATE: I can't read.

ATTORNEY: Do you have an opinion on this case?

CANDIDATE: What case are you talking about?

ATTORNEY: I'll accept this one for the jury.

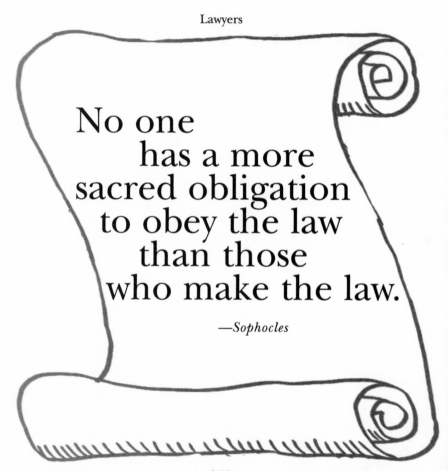

No one
has a more
sacred obligation
to obey the law
than those
who make the law.

—*Sophocles*

Of course, you can't take it with you,
but with taxes, funeral expenses,
and lawyers' fees, you can't
leave it behind either.

Between pigeons and politicians,
it's hard to keep the courthouse clean.

Pettifogger, n. A lawyer whose methods are petty, underhanded, or disreputable; one given to quibbling over trifles.

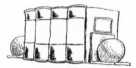

What is the only thing your lawyer isn't willing to make a postponement?

Your bill.

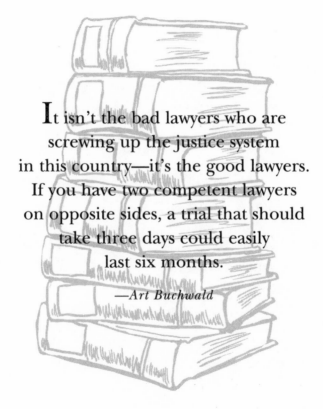

It isn't the bad lawyers who are
screwing up the justice system
in this country—it's the good lawyers.
If you have two competent lawyers
on opposite sides, a trial that should
take three days could easily
last six months.

—*Art Buchwald*

The judicial process is like a cow.
The public is gored on its horns,
the government has it by the tail,
and the lawyers are milking it.

Approaching a jury selection panel,
an obnoxious attorney quizzed the
potential jurors for a long time and finally
asked the question, "Do any of you here today
dislike lawyers?" After a long, awkward silence,
the judge was heard to state, "I do."

Strange but True

Lizzie Borden was actually acquitted of killing her father and stepmother.

Infants are prohibited in Los Angeles from dancing in public halls.

In Hawaii, it is illegal to put pennies in your ears.

Advertising on tombstones is outlawed in Roanoke, Virginia.

I tell the tale, which is strictly true,
Just by way of convincing you,
How very little since things were made
They have altered in the lawyer's trade.

—*Rudyard Kipling, "A Truthful Story"*

Lawyers are like physicians;
what one says, another contradicts.

—*Sholom Aleichem*

Win your lawsuit, lose your money.

They all laid their heads together
like as many lawyers when they are gettin'
ready to prove that a man's heirs ain't
got any right to his property.

—*Mark Twain*

When the president does it,
that means it is not illegal.

—*Richard Nixon*

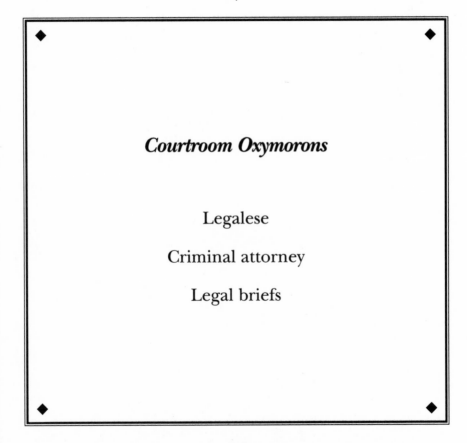

Courtroom Oxymorons

Legalese

Criminal attorney

Legal briefs

Q: What is the difference between
the dry cleaner and a lawyer?

A: The cleaner pays if it loses your suit.
A lawyer can lose your suit and still
take you to the cleaners.

On average in our cities,
there are 2.8 law enforcement employees
for every 1,000 citizens.

—*U.S. Department of Justice statistics bulletin*

Top Five Things that Sound Dirty in Law but Aren't

5. Is it a penal offense?

4. For $200 an hour, she'd better be good!

3. Have you looked through his briefs?

2. Can you get her to drop her suit?

1. Better leave the handcuffs on.

My strong point is weeping as I appeal
to the jury, and I seldom fail to clear my man.
Out of eleven murder cases last year
I cleared nine of the murderers. Having been
in jail no less than four times myself,
my experience cannot fail to prove
of value to my clients.
Come early and avoid the rush.

*—From a late-nineteenth-century legal advertisement
by attorney Major Hopkins*

The law is the only profession which records its mistakes carefully, exactly as they occurred, and yet does not identify them as mistakes.

—Eliot Dunlap Smith

God save us from the lawyer's "et cetera."

—French proverb

After hearing that the lesser charge
of manslaughter was defined as a killing
under the influence of sudden passion,
a prospective juror replied, "You're kidding.
I found my first husband in bed with
another woman and all I did was divorce him.
I had no idea I could have shot him."

Actual News Headlines

"Juvenile Court to Try Shooting Defendant"

"Drug Firm Ordered to Supply Women"

"Suicides Asked to Reconsider"

A Dublin lawyer died in poverty and
the townspeople approached the judge to
ask for a shilling to bury the man. "A shilling?!"
remarked the judge. "Here's a guinea.
Go bury twenty of them."

If you can't convince them,
confuse them.

—*Harry Truman*

Contingency fee: If the lawyer doesn't
win the suit, then the lawyer gets nothing.
If the lawyer wins the suit, then the plaintiff
gets nothing.

Lawyer: A cat who settles disputes
between mice.

A legal secretary took a call asking for a lawyer in the firm. "I'm sorry, sir, but that attorney died suddenly last night," was her regretful answer.

An hour later, the same person called for the deceased. "This is not a joke, sir, your ex-wife's attorney has passed away."

An hour later, he called again and the exasperated receptionist declared, "Sir, that attorney is dead! Why do you keep calling?" "I just love hearing that bit of news," was the answer.

A lawyer starts his career giving
$500 worth of law for $5 and ends giving
$5 worth for $500.

The acme of judicial distinction means
the ability to look a lawyer straight in the eye
for two hours and not hear a
damned word he says.

—*U.S. Supreme Court Chief Justice John Marshall*

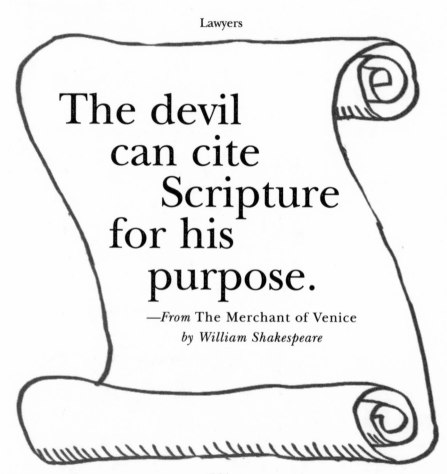

The devil
can cite
Scripture
for his
purpose.

—*From* The Merchant of Venice
by William Shakespeare

A lawyer stood before God in judgment, and God said, "To prove your worth, argue a point of law for me."

"I'm too nervous and ill-prepared to do that," responded the lawyer, "but I was always good at refuting in court. You argue a point of law, and I'll refute you."

A woman went to see a Broadway play in the heart of New York. When she sat down, she noticed the seat in front of her was vacant. She struck up a conversation with the man adjacent to the empty chair and learned he was a lawyer. She asked who might hold the ticket for the empty seat.

"I do," said the man.

The woman remarked what a pity it was for the ticket to go to waste and wondered why he didn't give it to a client or relative who would enjoy the play.

The lawyer answered, "Actually, several wanted to use the ticket, but they were all busy attending my wife's funeral."

Notable Law Practitioners Who Never Attended Law School

Patrick Henry (1736–1799),
member of the Continental Congress

John Marshall (1755–1835),
Supreme Court chief justice

William Wirt (1772–1834), attorney general

Abraham Lincoln (1809–1865), president

Stephen Douglas (1813–1861), Illinois senator

Strom Thurmond (1902–),
South Carolina senator

Four out of five doctors say that if they
were stranded on a deserted island with
no lawyers, they wouldn't need any aspirin.

Litigation is a machine which you go into
as a pig and come out as sausage.

—*Ambrose Bierce*

Experts are people who know much about a little and continue to learn more about less until they know everything about almost nothing.

Lawyers know a little about a lot, learning less about more until they know nothing about almost everything.

Judges begin knowing everything but end knowing nothing, owing to lawyers and experts.

A man walked into a bar with a crocodile and asked, "Do you serve lawyers here?"

"We sure do," the bartender answered.

"Good. I'll have a beer, and my croc will have a lawyer."

The worse the society, the more law there will be. In Hell there will be nothing but law and due process meticulously observed.

—*Grant Gilmore,* New York Times

"Now," said the lawyer, "are you sure you told me all the truth? For if I am to defend you I must know everything."

"Yep. Sure. I told you everything."

"Good. I think I can easily get you acquitted, for you have an excellent alibi that proves you are innocent, beyond a doubt, of this robbery. Now you are sure, absolutely sure, that you've told me everything?"

"Yeah. All except where I hid the money."

Strange but True

Ms. Roe in the famed case *Roe v. Wade*, which
basically legalized abortion in the United States,
now supports the antiabortion movement.

In Nevada, it's against the law for undertakers
to use profane language in the presence
of a corpse.

In the early 1900s, an elephant was tried,
convicted, and hanged for murdering
a politician's daughter during a circus parade.

In 1994, a Spaniard broke into his ex-girlfriend's car and shot himself dead. She then sued the man's family for damage to the interior of her car.

A jury numbering twelve members harkens back to the days when astrologers picked who would sit on a jury. In order to be fair to the defendant, it was believed that jury members representing each of the twelve zodiac signs would ensure a diversity of personalities to sit in judgment.

An Ohio man went to a lawyer to ask what
her smallest fee was. She answered,
"$100 for three questions." "Isn't that a lot
of money for just three questions?" he asked.
"Yes," she replied, "and what is your
third question?"

Lawyers and preachers and tomtits' eggs,
there are more of them hatched
than come to perfection.

—*Benjamin Franklin, from* Poor Richard's Almanac

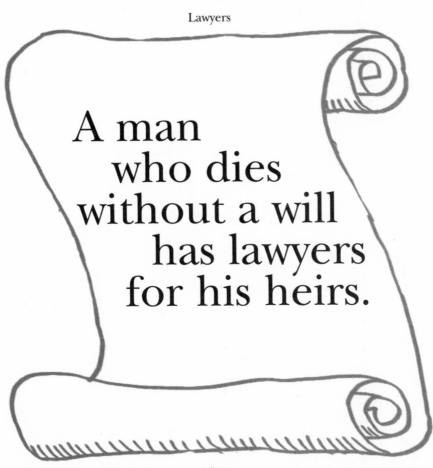

A man
who dies
without a will
has lawyers
for his heirs.

My code is lost.

—Napoleon, on hearing that a commentary had been written on his legal code

His clerk, assistant, housekeeper, secretary,
confidential plotter, adviser, intriguer,
and bill of costs increaser, Miss Brass—
a kind of amazon of common law.

—Charles Dickens, The Old Curiosity Shop

Tammany Hall saying:
More lawyers live on politics
than flies on a dead camel.

A woman sued a man for $5,000 because
the defendant swore at her in traffic, even
though he offered to meet with her and
apologize. She won $2,500 at the first court
trial but lost all on his appeal when she
failed to prove that her distress was more
than a reasonable person could endure.

It is the trade of lawyers to question
everything, yield nothing, and to talk
by the hour.

—*Thomas Jefferson*

In 1989, a prominent New York law firm
recorded revenues in the range of
$517.5 million, with an average partner share
of $1.2 million. 1992 revenues were down
to a mere $440 million with profits
per partner at only $885,000.

After examining the contents of his newly
instituted "Suggestion Box," the senior partner
of a large law firm was vexed. "Why can't
they say what they mean? Why are they
so vague? What 'kite'? Which 'lake'?"

Q: Why is it dangerous for lawyers to
walk onto a construction site when
plumbers are working?

A: The plumbers might connect
the drain line to the wrong suer.

Under Oath . . .

DEFENDANT: Judge, I want you to appoint another lawyer for me.

JUDGE: Why is that?

DEFENDANT: Because this public defender isn't interested in my case.

JUDGE, TO THE PUBLIC DEFENDER: Do you have any comments on the defendant's motion?

PUBLIC DEFENDER: Sorry, Your Honor, I wasn't listening.

LAWYER: The truth of the matter is that you were not an unbiased, objective witness, isn't it? You, too, were shot in the fracas, were you not?

WITNESS: No, sir. I was shot midway between the fracas and the belly button.

LAWYER: Are you qualified to give a urine sample?

WITNESS: Yes. I have been since early childhood.

If it wasn't for wills, lawyers would have
to go to work at an essential employment.

—*Will Rogers*

The people should fight for their law
as for their city wall.

–*Heraclitus*

LAWYER TO CLIENT: Which do you want first, bad news or worse news?

CLIENT: Give me the bad.

LAWYER: Your wife discovered a picture worth $400,000.

CLIENT: All right! What could be worse news?!

LAWYER: It was a picture of you and your secretary.

ATTORNEY: Would you be able to participate
   in an endeavor in which the final and
   ultimate result might be the demise of
   the aforementioned, and that due to a
   lethal injection?
PROSPECTIVE JUROR: I guess I could on a
   weekend.

The trial lawyer does what Socrates
was executed for: Making the worse
argument appear the stronger.

—*Judge Irving Kauffman*

Changing lawyers is like moving to a
different deck chair on the *Titanic*.

A Washington, D.C., physician, after being grilled in a medical malpractice trial, thought he'd hop in his Mercedes and drive away his frustration. He stopped for a drink in a Virginia tavern, where he growled out loud, "Lawyers! Damned bunch of horses' asses!"

"Hey, buddy," warned the bartender, "watch your mouth. This is horse country."

Amazing Courtroom Confessions

"In my attempt to kill a fly, I drove into a telephone pole."

"I had been driving for forty years when I fell asleep at the wheel and had an accident."

"I thought the window was down, but I found out it was up when I put my head through it."

Doctors purge the body,
preachers the conscience,
lawyers the purse.

—*German proverb*

A lawyer is a man who helps you
get what's coming to him.

—*Laurence J. Peter*

QUESTION: What is your name?
ANSWER: Mary Ann O'Donnell.
QUESTION: And what is your marital status?
ANSWER: Fair.

QUESTION: Why did you kick Mr. Brown in the crotch?
ANSWER: How could I have known that the guy was about to turn around?

A Scotsman went to a lawyer for advice and explained the details of the case. "Have you told me everything, precisely as the incident occurred?" asked the lawyer.

"Och, aye, sair, I thought it best to tell ye the plain truth. Ye can add the lies into it yourself."

Three surgeons were discussing their favorite type of patients. The first said, "I like librarians. When you cut them open, everything is located by a numbering system."

The second said, "I like engineers. All their parts are color coded."

The third surgeon said, "The easiest are lawyers. They have only two parts, their mouths and their rears, and both are interchangeable."

[Lawyers are] those who use the law as shoemakers use leather; rubbing it, pressing it, and stretching it with their teeth, all to the end of making it fit their purposes.

—*Louis XII*

QUESTION: When was the last time you saw Michael?

ANSWER: At his funeral.

QUESTION: Did he make any comments to you at that time?

Strange but True

Lorenzo Dow, a nineteenth-century evangelist, was on a preaching tour when he came to a small town one cold winter night. At the local general store he saw the town's lawyers gathered around the potbellied stove. Dow told the men about a recent vision in which he had been given a tour of hell, much like the traveler in Dante's *Inferno*. One of the lawyers asked what he had seen. "Very much what I see here," he said. "All of the lawyers gathered in the hottest place."

Saying the majority had made the same mistake twice before with disastrous results, a dissenting judge offered this footnote to his opinion: "There was an old saying where I grew up—You ain't learned nothing the second time a mule kicks you."

Charles Dickens's will contained a request
that those attending his funeral
"wear no scarf, cloak, black bow, long
hatband, or other such revolting absurdity."

Lawyers are like cobwebs, which
may catch small flies but let wasps and
hornets break through.

— *Jonathan Swift*

The Lord
giveth
and the feds
taketh away.

I know no method to secure the
repeal of bad or obnoxious laws so effective
as their astringent execution.

—*Ulysses S. Grant*

Old lawyers never die.
They just lose their appeal.

"You've cheated me!" shouted the client to her lawyer. "You've kept my case going for months just to get rich off the whole thing!"

"Some thanks I get," returned the lawyer. "And just when I was going to name my new yacht after you."

A young couple was killed in an automobile crash on the way to their wedding. At the gates of Heaven, they expressed a wish to be formally married. Peter asked them to wait and left to look for a minister. Three years later, the minister arrived and the couple was married. Not long after, the couple became dissatisfied with marriage and asked for a divorce. Peter was exasperated.

"You saw how long it took to get a minister up here to marry you! How long do you think it'll take to get a lawyer?"

Top Ten Least Convincing Alibis

10. I was out drinking beer and picking up babes with Richard Simmons.

9. Busy trying to get Connie Chung pregnant.

8. Home watching CBS prime time.

7. Playing Ping-Pong with Carol Channing (videotape of Dave and Carol playing Ping- Pong).

6. Out buying hams for the audience!

5. Was attending a PBS fund-raiser
with Newt Gingrich.

4. Spent entire weekend trying to suck
myself into a Pepsi bottle.

3. Hypnotized by the sound of
Casey Kasem's voice.

2. Alone in my room doing some of
that Joycelyn Elders stuff.

1. I'm Batman!

—*David Letterman, February 3, 1995*

If law school is so hard to get through,
how come there are so many lawyers?

—*Calvin Trillin*

How is a lawyer like a rabbi?
He studies the law and the profits.

Judges are the weakest link
in our system of justice.
They are also the most protected.

—Alan Dershowitz

A lawyer was asked to be a
Jehovah's Witness. He said he'd not seen
the accident and had to decline, but he
did offer to take the case.

There was never a deed so foul
that something couldn't be said for the guy.
That's why there's lawyers.

—*Attorney Melvin Belli*

If builders built buildings the way
lawyers write laws, the first woodpecker to
come along would destroy civilization.

If it weren't
for lawyers,
we wouldn't
need them.

An appeal is when ye ask [one] court
to show its contempt for another court.

—Finley Peter Dunne

Q: What do you get when you cross
a lawyer with a librarian?

A: All the information you need,
but you can't understand a word of it.

A preacher found a signboard about to be changed and wrote at the bottom, I pray for all. A lawyer came later and wrote under that, I plead for all. A doctor saw the comments and wrote beneath, I prescribe for all. A common citizen finished the work with a final, I pay for all.

Not long after a man's house burned to the ground, he consulted his lawyer on recouping his losses.

"I'm sure there'll be no problem," his attorney assured him. "What kind of coverage do you have?"

"Fire and theft," was the reply.

"Oh, sorry, but you're out of luck," his lawyer informed him. "It should have been fire or theft."

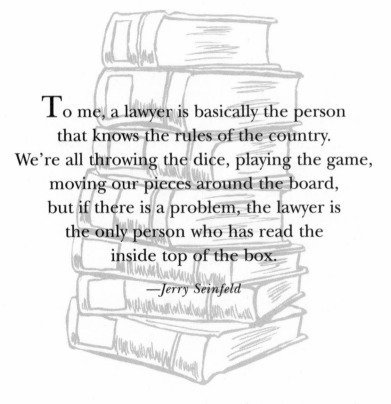

To me, a lawyer is basically the person
that knows the rules of the country.
We're all throwing the dice, playing the game,
moving our pieces around the board,
but if there is a problem, the lawyer is
the only person who has read the
inside top of the box.

—*Jerry Seinfeld*

"We can imagine no reason why,
with ordinary care, human toes could not
be left out of chewing tobacco, and if toes
are found in chewing tobacco, it seems to us
that somebody has been very careless."

—Pillars v. R. J. Reynolds Tobacco Co., *1918*

Fools and obstinate men make lawyers rich.

—*Henry George Bohn*

A corrupt lawyer found himself at the gates of Heaven with St. Peter reading to him all the self-serving and deceitful acts he had ever committed.

"You've done nothing for anyone in your entire life!" Peter accused.

The lawyer countered in his best legal posture, "Ha! Wrong! I once gave a dime to a wino and a nickel tip to a bellhop."

Peter turned to an angel and said, "Give this guy fifteen cents and tell him to go to hell."

Laws are generally found to be nets of
such a texture as the little creep through,
the great break through, and the
middle-sized are alone entangled in.

—*William Shenstone*

Two attorneys were vacationing in Africa on
safari. Upon hearing an approaching lion, they
panicked. One sat down and began removing
his shoes, saying, "I run better barefooted." The
other said, "You'll never outrun a lion!" The
other said, "No, I just have to outrun you."

A doctor and a lawyer were talking at a party where people repeatedly interrupted the doctor, asking him for medical advice.

The exasperated doctor asked the lawyer, "What do you do to stop people from asking legal advice when you're out of the office?"

The lawyer replied, "I give the advice and then send them a bill."

The doctor was shocked but decided to give it a try. The next day, the doctor wrote out the bills and took them to the mailbox. There he found a bill from the lawyer.

A defendant was asked if he wanted a bench trial or a jury trial. "Jury trial," he replied.

"Do you understand the difference?" asked the judge.

"Sure," replied the defendant. "That's where twelve ignorant people decide my fate instead of one."

FRASIER: I hate lawyers.
NILES: I do too, but they make wonderful
   patients. They have excellent health
   insurance and they never get better.

—From NBC's Frasier

A superstitious woman accidentally broke
a mirror in her house. She is expecting
seven years of bad luck, but her lawyer says
he thinks he can get it down to six.

———◆◆◆———

A teacher, an accountant, and a lawyer were asked, "How much is four plus four?"

The teacher answered, "Eight!"

The accountant said, "Seven or eight. I'll need to run that through my spreadsheet for verification."

The lawyer leaned forward and whispered, "How much do you want it to be?"

———◆◆◆———

PRISON VISITOR: How long are you in for?
PRISONER: Don't know, ma'am.
VISITOR: How can that be?
PRISONER: I got a life sentence.

A verbal contract isn't worth
the paper it's written on.

—*Samuel Goldwyn*

Strange but True

Renters in Rumford, Maine, are prohibited from biting landlords.

The words "insane" and "insanity" are not recognized medical terms but, rather, legal ones.

It's unlawful in Cushing, Oklahoma, to drink beer while in your underwear.

In Logan County, Colorado, a man is prohibited from kissing a sleeping woman without waking her first.

In 1994, a manic-depressive woman sued a Delaware hospital for $1.1 million. A judge ruled that hospital staff had been negligent in allowing her to gouge out her own eyes.

In Michigan, it's unlawful to play "The Star-Spangled Banner" for purposes of dancing.

A case was brought to court by a bus driver who declared his vehicle was struck late at night by a train that failed to give proper warning. The engineer protested that he was waving his lantern at the bus miles before the impact, and the railroad was exonerated. The lawyer for the engineer congratulated him on his convincing testimony.

"Thanks, but I sure was worried there for a while," said the engineer. "I was positive someone was going to ask me if the lantern was lit."

Question: According to the accident report,
you told the officer you had no injuries.
Answer: Well, when the officer arrived on the
scene, he saw that my horse was in such bad
shape that he shot it. When he came over
to me, and asked me how I was doing,
I immediately replied, "I'm okay!"

Lawyers are in the only profession where the
more there are, the more are needed.

—*Robert Lucky*

Two lawyers were walking along negotiating a case.

"Look," said one, "let's be honest with each other."

"Okay, you first," said the second. That was the end of the discussion.

DEFENSE ATTORNEY: You appear to have a great deal of knowledge in this matter, considering your educational background.

WITNESS: I'd return the compliment if I wasn't under oath.

A lawyer secretly approached the foreman of the jury and said, "It's worth $15,000 if you can get my client a verdict of manslaughter." The foreman winked and headed into the deliberations. When the verdict came back for manslaughter, the lawyer was delighted and slipped the cash to the foreman with words of congratulations. "It was not an easy verdict to get," admitted the foreman. "Everyone on the jury wanted an acquittal."

Old West Justice . . .

SLICKER: So they caught the murderer?
COWBOY: Yup.
SLICKER: Have they tried him yet?
COWBOY: Ain't had time. They only just got
through the lynching.

I used to be a lawyer,
but now I am a reformed character.

—*Woodrow Wilson*

How do you tell the difference between
a lawyer and a bulldog?

The bulldog generally has enough sense
to know when to let go.

One morning at the law office, one lawyer looked at the other and said, "You really look terrible this morning." His companion replied, "I woke up with a headache this morning and no matter what I try, I can't get rid of it." The first lawyer told him, "When that happens to me, I take a few hours off during the day to go home and make love with my wife. It always works for me." Later that afternoon, the first lawyer commented on his partner's improved appearance. "I took your advice and it worked," the partner replied. "By the way, you've got a beautiful house."

Q: You said the officer arrested you while you were quietly minding your own business?

A: Yes, Your Honor, he grabbed me by the collar, threw me to the ground, handcuffed me, and hauled me into the station.

Q: You were minding your own business, making no noise or disturbance of any kind?

A: None whatsoever.

Q: Strange. What's your business?

A: I'm a burglar.

Bless those men in the black robes.
They're in the same union with us.

—Attorney Melvin Belli, speaking of judges

A celebrated attorney, John Randolph,
met a personal enemy in the street one day
who refused to make way for him on the
sidewalk. "I never move aside for a rascal,"
said the man.

"I do," answered Randolph, and let him pass.

JUDGE: One year and a $50 fine.
DEFENDANT'S LAWYER: I would like to make a
     motion to have that sentence reversed.
JUDGE: All right, fifty years, and a $1 fine.

Q: What do you call a lawyer
who's gone bad?

A: A senator.

Q: How many lawyers does it take
to change a lightbulb?

A: You'll need 250 just to lobby
for the research grant.

Some laws of state aimed at curbing crime
are even more criminal.

—*Fredrich Engels*

WIDOW: Are you the judge of reprobate?
JUDGE: I am the judge of probate.
WIDOW: You're the one. My husband died
　　detested and left me several little infidels.
　　I want to be their executioner.

I regret that I have but one law firm
to give for my country.

—*Adlai Stevenson*

Under Oath . . .

JUDGE: Did you tell your lawyer that your husband had offered you indignities?

WITNESS: He didn't offer me nothing; he just said I could have the furniture.

LAWYER: Now, doctor, isn't it true that when a person dies in his sleep, in most cases he just passes quietly away and doesn't know anything about it until the next morning?

LAWYER: Are you married?
WITNESS: No, I'm divorced.
LAWYER: And what did your husband do before you divorced him?
WITNESS: A lot of things I didn't know about.

A lawyer found himself at the end of a long line stretching back from the pearly gates of Heaven. He was willing to wait his turn, but forty angels came to escort him to the front. He was flattered by the attention and asked St. Peter why he should be so honored. Peter replied, "Well, we totaled up your billable hours and found that you were 197 when you died!"

A judge and a lawyer were discussing the transmigration of souls into animals.

"Suppose you were to be turned into an animal—would you prefer to be an ass or a horse?"

"An ass, for sure," replied the lawyer. The judge was surprised. "Why?"

"I've heard of an ass being a judge, but a horse, never."

Strange but True

A man willed his body to Harvard for medical study, stipulating that his skin be fashioned into drumheads on which "Yankee Doodle" was to be played every June 17.

Napoleon's last will included bequests totaling six million francs, although he had no funds for the purpose.

In 1964, a jury awarded $50,000 to a woman who claimed a cable car accident in San Francisco had made her a nymphomaniac.

In 1993, a Wyoming woman filed suit against the widow of a man she had run over in her pickup. The lawsuit demanded compensation for the "grave and crippling psychological injuries" the woman suffered while watching the man die.

A lawyer and a physician had a dispute over who had precedence and asked Diogenes to settle the matter. The great man said, "Let the thief go first and the executioner to follow."

Q: What is the difference between a lawyer and God?

A: God doesn't think He's a lawyer.

Where there is a rift in the lute,
the business of the lawyer is to widen
the rift and gather the loot.

—*Arthur G. Hays*

Laws are inherited like diseases.

—*Goethe*

"Great news, Dad!" shouted the excited young attorney. He had been given his father's law practice and thought he could impress the old man. "I've managed to settle the old Scarlotti case! What do you think of that?"

"You've settled it?!" roared his father. "I gave that case to you as a lifetime annuity!"

What do you get when you cross
the Godfather with a lawyer?

An offer you can't understand.

Fond of lawsuits, little wealth;
fond of doctors, little health.

—*Hebrew proverb*

A petite lawyer, appearing as a witness in a messy divorce proceeding, was confronted by an ox of an opposing lawyer, who asked what she did for a living.

"I am an attorney," she said.

"Hey, little lady—I could pick you up and put you in my back pocket!" he laughed.

"Probably," was the reply, "but then you'd have more legal knowledge in your pants than you ever had in your head."

JUDGE TO JURY: What possessed you to acquit
the defendant? What reason could you
have had?
JURY FOREMAN: Insanity.
JUDGE: Not all twelve of you at the same time.

The only civil delinquents whose judge
must of necessity be chosen from
(amongst) themselves.

—*Charles Caleb Colton, defining lawyers*

Your lawyer in practice spends a considerable part of his life in doing distasteful things for disagreeable people who must be satisfied against an impossible time limit in which are hourly interruptions from other disagreeable people who want to derail the train; and for his blood, sweat, and tears, he receives in the end a few unkind words to the effect that it might have been done better, and a protest at the size of the fee.

—*William L. Prossner*

"Do you remember," asked the young attorney, "when you said I'd never be rich? Well, it looks like I'm on the road to riches at last."

"I never said you wouldn't be rich," said the older gentleman. "I said you'd never have money of your own, and I still say so."

My daddy is a movie actor and sometimes
he plays the good guy and sometimes
he plays the lawyer.

—*Harrison Ford's son*

WIFE: You just don't care anymore!

HUSBAND: You're upset. Let's buy you something to make you feel better.

WIFE: Like what?

HUSBAND: How about a trip to the Orient?

WIFE: No.

HUSBAND: A BMW?

WIFE: No.

HUSBAND: Well, what do you want?

WIFE: A divorce.

HUSBAND: I wasn't planning on spending that much.

LAWYER: You have an excellent case, ma'am.

CLIENT: But a friend of mine said he had an exactly similar case, and you were the lawyer on the other side, and you beat him.

LAWYER: Yes, I remember, but I'll see to it that those games aren't played in court this time around.

Apologists for the profession contend
that lawyers are as honest as other men,
but this is not very encouraging.

—Ferdinand Lundberg

LAWYER FOR THE DEFENSE: Remember you are under oath.

WITNESS: Don't I know it! I'm telling the truth for nothing when I could have had $150 by lying for your side of the case, as you well know.

FRIEND: Who was the lawyer who defended you in your recent case?

PLAINTIFF: It wasn't a lawyer, it was a counselor-at-law.

FRIEND: What's the difference?

PLAINTIFF: About $150 an hour.

Strange but True

In Gary, Indiana, it is against the law to attend
the theater within four hours of eating garlic.

In Massachusetts, it's illegal to manufacture,
sell, or knowingly use an exploding golf ball.

In Toledo, Ohio, it's illegal to throw
any type of reptile at another person.

In Washington, D.C., it is unlawful
to marry your mother-in-law.

By law, Kentuckians must bathe
at least once a year.

No brilliance is needed in the law.
Just common sense, and relatively
clean fingernails.

—John Mortimer

A lawyer is someone who approaches
every subject with an open mouth.

LAWYER: Sir, isn't it true that on December 23 of last year you were caught wearing a sequined strapless gown after climbing to the top of the park fountain, where you did an imitation of Uncle Miltie reciting the Gettysburg address, all the while blowing kisses at every passerby?

DEFENDANT: I'm not sure. What did you say the date was?

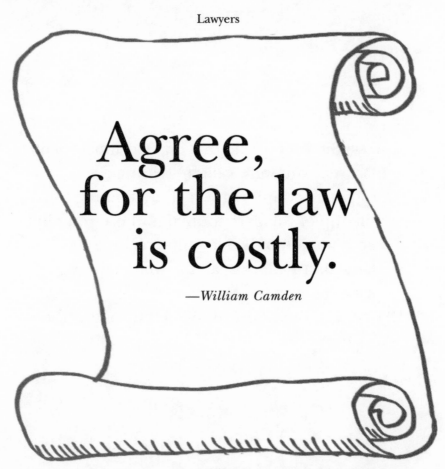

Agree, for the law is costly.

—*William Camden*

Some lawyers get confused when
they try to remember if they were born
in a log cabin or a manger.

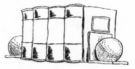

A tiger wandered upon a pile of elephant
dung, took a bite, and spit it out. He proceeded
to do this over and over until a concerned elephant approached and asked what his problem
was.

"I just ate a lawyer," was the reply, "and I
can't get the taste out of my mouth."

Under Oath . . .

LAWYER: So, you are unconscious, and they pulled you from the bucket. What happened then?

WITNESS: Mr. Steward gave me artificial insemination. You know, mouth to mouth.

LAWYER: She had three children, right?
WITNESS: Yes.
LAWYER: How many were boys?
WITNESS: None.
LAWYER: Were there any girls?

COURTROOM QUESTION: When he went, had you gone and had she, if she wanted to and were able, for the time being excluding all the restraints on her not to go, gone also, would he have brought you, meaning you and she, with him to the station?

OPPOSING COUNSEL: Objection, Your Honor. That question should be taken out and shot.

A guy who sets out to make a name
for himself as a lawyer usually gets to
hear plenty of other names directed at him
along the way.

God works wonders now and then;
Behold a lawyer, an honest man.

—*Benjamin Franklin*

Defense counsel: So if I hit the prosecutor
at this very moment and he fell over the
back of this railing, hit his head, and a
subdural hematoma immediately began to
form, the blood that was leaking into the
space beneath his skull would have essentially
the same components as the blood leaking
into his teeny little brain?

Be you never so high, the law is above you.

—*Thomas Fuller*

Warning Signs that You Need a New Lawyer

You met him in prison.

All his law books are by Time-Life.

During your initial consultation, he tries
to sell you Amway.

He tells you that his last good case
was Budweiser.

When the prosecutors see who your lawyer is,
they high-five each other.

Lawyers

He picked the jury by playing
Duck, Duck, Goose.

During the trial, you catch him playing
with his Gameboy.

He asks a hostile witness to "pull my finger."

A prison guard is shaving your head.

—*On a T-shirt, copyright 1993, Jack Thomas, ex-attorney*

Q: Why did the lawyer cross the road?

A: To sue the chicken on the other side.

Litigant, n. A person about to give up his skin for the hope of retaining his bones.

—*Ambrose Bierce*

A lawyer charged a man $500 for legal services. The man paid with crisp new $100 bills. After the client left, the lawyer found that two bills had stuck together and he'd been overpaid by $100.

"This is a real ethical dilemma," the lawyer said to himself. "Should I tell my partner?"

There is plenty of law
at the end of a nightstick.

—*Grover A. Whalen*

It took man thousands of years
to put words down on paper,
and his lawyers still wish he hadn't.

—*Mignon McLaughlin*

It ain't no sin if you crack a few laws
now and then, just so long as you
don't break any.

—*Mae West*

Q: What do you call an automobile accident between two lawyers?

A: A Saab story.

Two wrongs don't make a right,
but they often appear the next best thing
in legal disputes or tangles with lawyers.

—*Deborah L. Rhode*

Society holds trials for the same reason
that Shakespeare had comic relief in
Macbeth. So (if you're on trial) try to make
everyone laugh. Pleading innocent is
usually the best way to do this.

—*P. J. O'Rourke*

Justice is incidental to law and order.

—*J. Edgar Hoover*